Young Children's

Mix and Fix Cook Book

Young Children's

Mix and Fix Cook Book

Published By
PARENTS' MAGAZINE ENTERPRISES, INC.
For
PLAYMORE, INC.
New York, New York

Contents

A Note for Parents

Here in YOUNG CHILDREN'S MIX AND FIX COOKBOOK are easy-to-follow recipes created especially for the very young chef. What child hasn't wanted to try his hand in the kitchen! Boys as well as girls feel the urge to cook in these times when men are getting into the act with their barbecue specialties and skillet skills. The problem is to find recipes youngsters can use. Too often your own cookbooks are impossible for a child to follow.

YOUNG CHILDREN'S MIX AND FIX COOKBOOK gives your child the pride of owning his own book. All the recipes are designed for the younger child, although there is no age limit to the enjoyment of the finished product. The number of ingredients in each recipe is limited, and the directions involve only a few easy steps. With the help of this book, most children will soon enjoy preparing their own snacks and even simple dishes for breakfast or lunch.

Your youngster's success in following these child-geared recipes may well develop into a life-long interest in cooking as a rewarding and pleasureable skill, whether as a weekend chef or a full-time gourmet cook. And lagging appetites can be spurred when youngsters are allowed to prepare their own snacks.

The recipes in this book have been carefully selected and edited by the editors of HUMPTY DUMPTY'S MAGAZINE, published by Parents' Magazine Enterprises, Inc. While primarily designed to entertain children, HUMPTY DUMPTY also offers educational values through its carefully developed articles, stories and poems, and in its varied features on music, art, science and other stimulating, activities. This dual emphasis is reflected in YOUNG CHILDREN'S MIX AND FIX COOKBOOK.

A Guide for Young Cooks

Cooking is fun, but as in many fun things, there are rules to be followed. The first rule is to pick the right time. When Mother is getting ready to fix dinner is not a good time for you to make a snack. But a rainy Saturday morning would be a perfect time to fix a cheerful dessert. The next rule is to ask Mother if it's all right for you to use the kitchen. Make sure she or some other grown-up is with you; never, never use the stove or broiler or toaster when you are alone.

When you have permission to cook, read the recipe carefully. Do you understand all the steps? If not, ask for help. Next make sure you have all the ingredients the recipe calls for. You can't make Cool-as-a-Cucumber sandwiches if you don't have any cucumbers in the house!

Have Mom or Dad remove hot pots and pans from the stove for you; don't do it yourself. Bread is hot when it comes from the toaster, so be careful and avoid burned fingers. Make sure all pot handles are turned away from the front of the stove; otherwise it's too easy to accidentally knock them over. But don't turn the handle so that it's over another pot that may also be on the stove or it will get too hot to touch.

Wash your hands thoroughly before you start to cook. And wear an apron to protect your clothes from spills. Perhaps the most important rule that every good cook follows is to clean up the kitchen as soon as you're finished. Wash the utensils you've used, return remaining ingredients to the closet or refrigerator, hang up dishtowels and brush away crumbs. If you spill something on the floor, wipe it up immediately. When Mother sees how professional you are, you won't have any difficulty getting permission to cook as often as you wish.

Sandwiches

Many years ago, an Englishman was so fond of playing cards that he wouldn't even take time out to eat his meals. He ordered that his food should be brought to him, prepared in such a way that he could conveniently eat it with his fingers. His cook put some meat between two slices of bread, and that's how the sandwich was born. The man was the Earl of Sandwich, and this extremely popular type of meal bears his name to this day.

But there's more to sandwiches than meat and bread. They can be open——just bread on the bottom ——they can be hot and they can be made with salads or jams or special butters or anything at all that pleases your fancy. When they're served hot or open, they are eaten with a knife and fork. When the filling is moist, as in a tuna salad sandwich, they should be eaten as soon as they are made. But you can always prepare the filling in advance, refrigerate it if necessary, and spread it on the bread when you're ready to eat.

Sandwiches can be made with all kinds of bread and rolls; toasted or not. You can get interesting new tastes by using pumpernickel bread instead of white bread, or try rye or whole wheat for a change. Seeded rolls, soft rolls——they all make delicious sandwiches. Hamburger and frankfurter buns can also be used for fillings other than ground beef patties and hot dogs.

For a quick lunch that's also good for you, a sandwich with a meat, cheese or fish filling, with lettuce and tomato added, plus a tall glass of milk and fruit will keep you going until dinner.

Make a sandwich for yourself, plus an extra one for your Mother or a friend. Impress Dad by fixing lunch for the two of you, or show your big sister how much you appreciate her helping you with your homework by fixing some Fancy Hot Dogs for both of you.

Banana Butter Sandwiches

What makes peanut butter better?
Bananas, of course!

WHAT YOU NEED

Peanut butter • 4 slices of bread
1 ripe banana • Butter or margarine

HOW TO FIX

1. Spread 2 slices of bread with peanut butter.
2. Slice bananas. Place slices over the spread peanut butter.
3. Butter the 2 remaining slices of bread, and place over the bottom slices of bread. Eat right away.

This makes 2 sandwiches.

TUNA
TREASURE BOATS

Watch out for pirates
when you make these treasure boats!

WHAT YOU NEED

1 can tuna
¼ cup pickle relish
¼ cup mayonnaise
4 unsliced hot dog buns
2 slices American cheese
Pretzel sticks

HOW TO FIX

1. Mix tuna, pickle relish and mayonnaise.
2. Hollow out center of buns.
3. Spoon tuna filling in hollow of buns.
4. Cut cheese diagonally, then fit each triangle of cheese on a pretzel stick to make a sail.
5. Stick sail into tuna-filled boats.

Ahoy there! Four tuna treasure boats for you and your friends!

stan tuson

TRIPLE-TREAT SANDWICHES

Combine the tastes you like the most.
That's what makes this sandwich so good.
Try one with a bowl of soup.

WHAT YOU NEED:
2 slices white bread
1 tablespoon softened cream cheese
1 slice whole wheat bread
1 tablespoon honey

HOW TO FIX:

1. Spread slice of white bread with cream cheese.
2. Place whole wheat slice on top.
3. Spread honey on whole wheat slice.
4. Cover with remaining slice of white bread.
5. Cut the three-layer sandwich in half from corner to corner, making two triangles. Cut each triangle in half again, making 4 triangle-shaped pieces for easy eating.

    Some other combinations you can use are:

    Peanut butter and jelly or jam;

    Cold cuts and cheese spread;

    Cheese spread and deviled ham.

FANCY HOT DOGS

Here's a delicious lunch suggestion for a snowy afternoon.
Ask an adult to help you plan and prepare —

FANCY HOT DOGS.

WHAT YOU NEED

1 hot dog

2 toothpicks

1 slice of bacon

1 slice of American cheese

WHAT TO DO

1. Carefully make a cut down the hot dog — but don't cut all the way through!

2. Cut the cheese to fit into the slit you just made.

3. After the cheese is in the hot dog, wrap bacon around it to hold in the cheese.

4. Hold the bacon secure at each end with a toothpick.

5. Place in a baking pan and bake in a hot oven (400°F.) until the bacon is crisp.

It may be cold outside, but your lunch will be hot!

COOL-AS-A-CUCUMBER SANDWICHES

Wishing for a cool lunch on a hot day? A cucumber sandwich makes you feel icely very nicely!

WHAT YOU NEED

1 cucumber

4 slices white bread

Mayonnaise

Salt and pepper

HOW TO FIX

1. Keep cucumber cold in refrigerator until you are ready to eat. Then ask a grownup to help you peel it. Slice 8 thin slices.

2. Spread 2 slices of bread with butter. Spread the other 2 slices with mayonnaise.

3. Place 4 slices of cucumber on each slice of mayonnaise-spread bread.

4. Sprinkle — very lightly — with salt and pepper.

5. Cover with the buttered bread slices. Cut each sandwich into quarters so that each quarter has a piece of cucumber inside. *This makes 2 servings.*

SUNSHINE
SANDWICHES

Who *doesn't* like peanut butter? Here's a
new kind of peanut butter sandwich you can make!

WHAT YOU NEED

¼ cup undiluted frozen orange juice concentrate
½ cup peanut butter   8 slices bread, your favorite kind

HOW TO FIX

1. Put the undiluted orange juice concentrate and peanut butter in a small bowl, and mix with a fork until well blended.

2. Spread the peanut butter mixture on four slices of bread.

3. Top with remaining slices, cut in half, and serve with a sunshiney smile.

This recipe makes 4 sandwiches.

TOASTED
DEVIL CHEESE
SANDWICH

This zesty sandwich will
perk up your lunchtime.

WHAT YOU NEED:

2 slices bread

1 slice American cheese

1½ tablespoons deviled ham spread

HOW TO FIX:

1. Toast the bread.
2. Spread mustard on one slice. Top with cheese slice.
3. Spread deviled ham on the remaining slice of toast.
4. Put the sandwich together. Cut in half.

Makes 1 sandwich.

stan tusan

TUNA-CHEESE
SANDWICH SPREAD

Cheesey tuna sandwiches are good
with a mug of tomato soup for lunch.

WHAT YOU NEED:

1 package (8 oz.) cream cheese
2 tablespoons milk
1 can (7 oz.) flaked tuna
  Bread or rolls

HOW TO FIX:

1. Let cream cheese stand at room temperature until it is soft.
2. Mix cream cheese and milk together in a bowl.
3. Drain liquid from tuna, then add tuna to the cream cheese mixture. Mix well.
4. Spread tuna-cheese mixture on bread, toast or rolls.

CRUNCHY DEVILS

Your family will think you're devilishly
clever to surprise them with
these sandwiches for lunch!

stan tusan

WHAT YOU NEED:

2 packages (3 ounces each) cream cheese, softened

1 can (2¼ ounces) deviled ham

¼ cup chopped peanuts

1 can (1 pound) brown bread with raisins

¼ cup apple jelly

HOW TO FIX

1. In a mixing bowl mix together cream cheese and deviled ham until smooth.

2. Stir in peanuts.

3. Cut brown bread into 12 slices.

4. Spread cheese-ham mixture on 6 slices of bread.

5. Spread apple jelly on the other 6 slices.

6. Put together two slices (one spread with cheese-ham, one with jelly), making in all 6 sandwiches.

7. Cut sandwiches in half and serve.

PEANUT BUTTER
and JELLY
FRENCH TOAST

This tasty sandwich is good
for breakfast or lunch.

WHAT YOU NEED:

1 egg
¼ cup milk
4 slices white bread
　Peanut butter
　Jelly (grape or any flavor you like)

HOW TO FIX:

1. Break egg into a large shallow bowl. Beat egg with a fork, then stir in milk.

2. Spread 2 slices of bread with peanut butter, then spread jelly on top of the peanut butter. Top each with another slice of bread.

3. Dip sandwiches into the egg-milk mixture.

4. Cook on buttered griddle or skillet until brown on one side, then turn over and brown on other side.

5. Serve hot with a spoonful of jelly on top of each sandwich. Eat with a knife and fork.

Beverages

Things you drink can quench your thirst, cool you off and, sometimes, provide you with a meal. Creating your own beverages is much more fun than simply opening a bottle and pouring the contents into a glass. And often drinking something is a lot more fun than eating it! For example, if you think you don't like eggs, try Super Eggnog. If you don't care for milk, Taffy Tonic will show you just how marvelous it can be!

When you're combining ice cream with liquids, it will be easier if you take it out of the freezer, measure the amount you need and let it stand at room temperature until it's soft. Then it will mix faster and more thoroughly.

Beverages that include carbonated sodas—ginger ale, club soda, colas, and so forth—should be served immediately or you'll lose the fun of the bubles. When the recipe calls for a tall glass, it will be easier to handle if you use a straw. And if a scoop of ice cream is added, an iced teaspoon will help you get every bit of it from the glass to your mouth!

Don't forget that paper and plastic cups can be used instead of glasses. And if you have to mix several ingredients in the glass, hold it firmly with one hand while you stir with the other.

Now would be a good time for you to learn how to use some of the appliances Mother may have in the kitchen. A rotary egg beater makes great eggnogs, and so does an electric mixer or a blender. These are easy to use, once you learn how. But don't try them unless Mother is there to give you a hand. Even if you like to watch her when she's using her electric mixer, don't think you can do it all by yourself. There's skill involved in knowing the right way to handle appliances.

An important part of cooking is serving what you've fixed nicely, especially when you've invited a friend to share your treat with you. Put the glass on a saucer; it's neater and gives you a place to rest your spoon or straw. A napkin on the side will help you remove any "moustaches" that may appear after you've had a Purple Cow or a Valentine Float.

If you're serving a hot beverage ——soup in a mug, for example—— be sure to include a spoon. Some people can't drink very hot liquids comfortably, and a spoon makes it easier for them to manage.

Sometimes you want to help out with the refreshments for your own birthday party. What could be easier than preparing a tasty beverage for your guests? Just assemble enough glasses for everyone and mix up a Fruit Crush. The recipe on page 36 will make enough for you and five friends. Or use six scoops of ice cream and six small bottles of root beer and make Sippy Sodas for your guests. Just remember to count yourself when you're mixing and fixing for a crowd!

VALENTINE
APPLE JUICE

For a cold winter day, you can
have this apple drink warm.

WHAT YOU NEED

2 cups apple juice
1 tablespoon cinnamon red hots
1 teaspoon lemon juice

HOW TO FIX

1. Combine apple juice, red hots and lemon juice in sauce-pan.
2. Place saucepan over low heat, stirring with a wooden spoon until all the red hots melt.
3. Let cool a little, then serve warm in cups. Or, if you like it cold, chill and pour over ice cubes in glasses.

FRUIT CRUSH

On a hot day did you ever wish you could eat a snow-ball? Here's a frosty glassful that's even better!

WHAT YOU NEED

1 package of frozen, sweetened raspberries
2 bananas
1 6-ounce can of frozen grapefruit juice concentrate

HOW TO FIX

1. About an hour before you start making the Crush take the frozen grapefruit juice concentrate out of the freezer and let it stand at room temperature.
2. Put the frozen raspberries into a bowl.
3. Slice the bananas and add them to the bowl.
4. Add the partly thawed grapefruit juice concentrate to the bowl.
5. Let everything stand at room temperature for about an hour.
6. Spoon into sherbet glasses, and serve with spoons.
This recipe makes 6 servings.

SUPER EGGNOG

You'll want to join the holiday fun
by making eggnog for your family.

WHAT YOU NEED

2 eggs
2 tablespoons honey
2 cups cold milk
½ teaspoon vanilla extract
Nutmeg

HOW TO FIX

1. Beat eggs with beater until smooth and thick, then beat in honey.
2. Beat in milk and vanilla.
3. Pour into 2 glasses, then sprinkle each with a dash of nutmeg.

PEACH-HONEY DELIGHT

You'll feel like you're floating on a cloud
after fixing and sipping on a
Peach-honey Delight!
     Nutritious . . . Delicious.

WHAT YOU NEED

1 cup cold water
3 tablespoons strained peaches (baby food is ideal)
1 tablespoon honey
¼ cup nonfat dry milk

HOW TO FIX

1. In a shaker or a large glass jar with a top, combine water, peaches and honey. Sprinkle in the dry milk. Shake well.

2. Pour into a glass for one large serving—or divide the Peach-Honey Delight into two glasses and share one with a friend.

A delight fit for an angel!

stan tusan

BANANA MILK SHAKE

You'll be able to turn all sorts of monkeyshines after fixing and drinking a shake with bananas!

WHAT YOU NEED

1 ripe banana   1 cup cold milk
      1 scoop vanilla ice cream

HOW TO FIX

1. Blend the banana and the milk together in an electric blender. If you do not have a blender then mash the banana and mix in the milk till smooth.
2. Add 1 scoop of ice cream and blend together till the mixture is smooth, but still thick.
3. Pour into a tall glass.

Actually there should be enough
for you to share with a friend
if you use small glasses.

SIPPY SODA

Sip the soda,
spoon the ice cream,
to make your day complete!

WHAT YOU NEED

1 scoop of vanilla ice cream
1 small bottle of ice cold root beer
a tall glass *and* a long spoon *and* a straw, of course

HOW TO FIX

1. Put a scoop of vanilla ice cream into the tall glass.
2. Slowly add the root beer—don't let it foam over the top of the glass!
3. Now you're ready to sip and spoon.

stan tusan

YUMMY LEMON-ORANGE COOLER

Cool as a penguin
  Floating on ice.
You'll enjoy this frosty treat
Because it's extra nice!

stan tusan

WHAT YOU NEED

1/3 cup undiluted frozen orange juice concentrate, thawed

3 tablespoons honey   4 ice cubes

2 cups milk   1 pint lemon sherbet

HOW TO FIX

1. Combine orange juice concentrate and honey. Stir till well mixed.
2. Add milk; mix well.
3. Pour into a jar with the ice cubes. Cover and shake very well while counting to 30.
4. Spoon sherbet into four tall glasses.
5. Fill the glasses with the orange mixture.

Now serve at once to any friends (or penguins) who may be waiting for a taste!

GRAPE FLOAT

This super float is a good
afternoon snack or bedtime treat.

WHAT YOU NEED:

2 cups grape juice
2 scoops vanilla ice cream
Frozen whipped topping
Maraschino cherries

HOW TO FIX:

1. Pour grape juice into two tall glasses.
2. Add a scoop of ice cream to each glass.
3. Top each float with a spoonful of whipped topping and a maraschino cherry.
4. Serve each grape float with a straw and a long-handled spoon.

Makes two grape floats.

stan tusan

ORANGE EGGNOG

Christmas is a time for eggnog,
all kinds of eggnog, including this
recipe for *orange* eggnog!

WHAT YOU NEED

1 cup of cold milk   1 tablespoon confectioners' sugar

1 egg   ¼ teaspoon vanilla flavoring

½ cup of cold orange juice

WHAT TO DO

1. Mix all the ingredients together in a bowl.

2. Now, beat the mixture with an eggbeater or at low speed of an electric mixer until the mixture is thoroughly blended and foamy.

3. Pour eggnog into a glass and drink it up!
   There should be enough to share with a friend.

stan tusan

TAFFY BANANA DRINK

Rich, ripe bananas—a flavorful taffy—
One drink, and you'll say—"How deliciously daffy!"

WHAT YOU NEED

2 ripe bananas
4 tablespoons molasses
dash of salt
3 cups milk

HOW TO FIX

1. Thoroughly mash the bananas with a fork in a wide bowl.
2. Stir in the molasses and salt.
3. Gradually add the milk, mixing well each time before adding more milk.
4. Pour into tall glasses and serve.
This recipe makes 4 servings.

stan tusan

VALENTINE
FLOAT

Here's a Valentine's Day treat as pretty as it tastes. It'll make you say — "Sip-ly delicious!"

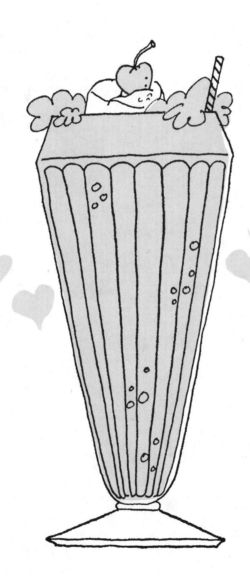

WHAT YOU NEED

1 pint of strawberry (or cherry) ice cream

1 quart of strawberry (or cherry) soda

4 marshmallows

4 maraschino cherries

HOW TO FIX

1. Put a large scoop of ice cream, partially melted, in the bottom of a large, tall glass.

2. Pour in a small amount of soda, and stir until partly blended. Leave some small lumps of ice cream to float in the drink.

3. Pour in more soda, to nearly fill the glass.

4. Using a butter knife or spoon handle, make a little slit in a marshmallow. Push a cherry into the slit just deep enough to keep it on top of the marshmallow.

5. With a spoon, set the marshmallow lightly on the surface of the float.

6. Repeat these steps to fill four glasses in all. Serve with straws and iced-teaspoons.

This makes 4 floats.

GRAPE-BANANA COOLER

What's cool, and fizzes, and gives you
a purple mustache? Try this and see!
(If you don't like mustaches, use a straw.)

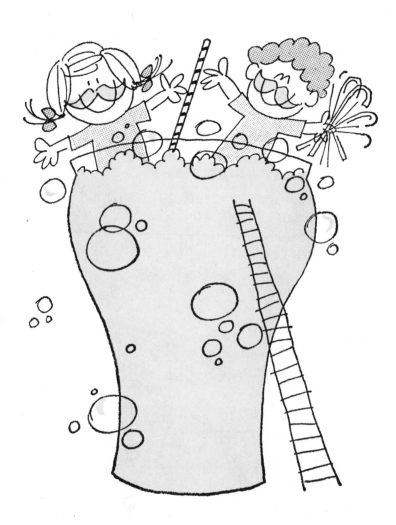

WHAT YOU NEED

1 bottle (24 ounces) grape juice, chilled
4 scoops banana ice cream
Club soda, chilled

HOW TO FIX

1. Use 4 tall glasses. Pour in grape juice to half-fill each glass.
2. Float a scoop of ice cream in each glass.
3. Fill glasses with club soda. Stir lightly.
Serve with iced-tea spoons.

This recipe makes 4 coolers.

stan tusan

TAFFY TONIC

In Great-Grandma's time, children drank sulphur-
and-molasses Spring Tonic. Here's an updated version.

WHAT YOU NEED

2 tablespoons molasses

Milk

1 scoop vanilla ice cream

Carbonated water (club soda)

HOW TO FIX

1. Put molasses into a tall glass.

2. Pour milk into the glass so it's half full.

3. Add ice cream. Stir vigorously with a spoon.

4. Fill to top with carbonated water. Stir just enough to mix the liquids.

5. Serve with an iced-teaspoon and a straw.

Makes one glass of Taffy Tonic.

PURPLE
COW

Nothing tastes better on a hot day
than a purple cow, or an orange cow,
or a brown cow.

WHAT YOU NEED:

Vanilla ice cream
Grape soda

HOW TO FIX:

1. Put 2 scoops of vanilla ice cream in a tall glass.
2. Fill the glass to the top with cold grape soda.
3. Stir to a pleasing purple.
If you would like an *orange cow*, use orange soda instead of grape soda. If you would like a *brown cow*, use root beer or cola.

Cookies, Candies, Desserts and Snacks

Everyone enjoys a between-meal snack, and youngsters like you need one to restore the energy you burn up in active play. But snacks can also be made with nourishing ingredients that contribute to the vitamins and minerals you need every day. And making your own snacks not only takes a load off Mother's shoulders, but it's fun! Some of the recipes in this section would even make perfect desserts for your friends.

The important thing to remember about snacks is that they are an extra treat; they are not substitutes for meals. Halfway between breakfast and lunch, or halfway between lunch and dinner, is snacktime. Or if you feel a little hungry at bedtime, then a quick snack would be just the thing to have. But when the clock says it's time for a regular meal, forget about having something sweet.

You'll find several recipes for sundaes, those delicious treats made with ice cream topped with various types of good things. Since you can enjoy them any day of the week, have you ever wondered why they're called sundaes? It happened this way. Years and years ago, ice cream sodas were not allowed to be sold on Sundays in a small town in the Middle West. A man who owned an ice cream parlor thought this was unfair, but he didn't want to break the law. So he started serving his customers ice cream and syrup——two of the ingredients in ice cream sodas—— and leaving out the third ingredient, soda water. His customers liked them so much that they ordered them whether it was Sunday or not.

Today you don't have to go to an ice cream parlor when you want a sundae; you can make one at home. Sundaes can be as plain or as fancy as you wish. Once you've tried the recipes for sundaes in this book, you may want to create your own variations. That's one of the fun things about learning to cook. Once you've become familiar with the basics, you can be as creative and as imaginative as you want to.

If possible, serve ice cream desserts after they've been at room temperature for about ten minutes or so. If you eat it straight from the freezer, you can't really taste the flavor of the ice cream; all you can taste is cold. Of course the ice cream shouldn't be allowed to get so soft that it runs all over the plate, but it shouldn't be hard as a rock, either.

Fruit is another excellent snack and dessert ingredient. If possible, use fresh fruits. But canned and frozen fruits are equally good. And don't forget dried fruits, such as prunes, raisins and apricots. They have a special flavor all their own and a tangy sweetness that's a perfect pick-me-up when you come home from school.

Share your cookies, candies, desserts and snacks with your family and friends. They will appreciate your thoughtfulness and they will certainly be impressed with your skill as a cook!

TROPICAL TREAT

A delicious dessert, especially for parties.

WHAT YOU NEED:

1 can (8 oz.) mandarin orange sections, chilled
1 can (8 oz.) pineapple tidbits
½ cup miniature marshmallows
1 pint heavy cream, whipped

HOW TO FIX:

1. Drain the liquid from the orange sections and pineapple tidbits.
2. Mix the fruit and marshmallows together in a large bowl.
3. Add enough whipped cream to thickly cover the fruit.
4. Gently mix the cream and the fruit together.
   Makes 4 to 6 servings.

stan tusan

59

BUTTERSCOTCH STACKS

They're so easy to fix and good to eat.
Stack them high
for a yummy dessert or snack.

WHAT YOU NEED

1 package (about 4 ozs.) instant
    butterscotch pudding
2 cups milk
15 graham crackers
    Whipped topping (the kind that squirts
      from a can)
    Chopped nuts

HOW TO FIX

1. Beat pudding mix and milk together until smooth, about one minute.

2. Spread pudding on graham cracker, then top with another cracker. Spread on more pudding, then top with another cracker. (Save extra pudding for dessert another day.)

3. Top each dessert with a squirt of whipped topping, then sprinkle chopped nuts on top.

Makes 5 butterscotch stacks.

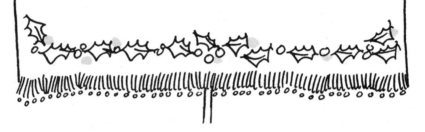

SNOWY COCONUT
TREATS

Now *you* can join the kitchen fun with
an easy-to-make recipe.

WHAT YOU NEED

2 tablespoons soft butter or margarine
½ cup brown sugar
2 tablespoons flaked coconut
6 graham crackers

HOW TO FIX

1. Blend sugar into butter and mix until smooth.
2. Mix in the coconut.
3. Spread mixture on the graham crackers.
4. Place the Treats on a sheet of aluminum foil and toast under the broiler until golden brown.

stan tusan

PORCUPINES

Porcupine candies are a great snack
with a glass of cold milk.

WHAT YOU NEED:

1 cup creamy peanut butter
½ cup sweetened condensed milk
¼ cup confectioners' sugar
½ cup finely chopped salted peanuts

HOW TO FIX:

1. In a bowl, blend peanut butter, condensed milk and confectioners' sugar together thoroughly with a wooden spoon, then knead with your hands.
2. Divide the candy mixture into small pieces. Roll each piece into a ball about 1" in diameter, then roll candy balls in chopped peanuts.

Makes about 24 candies.

stan tusan

PEPPERMINT CANDY SNOWBALLS

A snowball for me,

a snowball for you.

Don't wait for winter

to make these snowballs.

WHAT YOU NEED:

Vanilla ice cream
Crushed peppermint candy
Shredded coconut (if desired)
Chocolate sauce

HOW TO FIX:

1. Make ice-cream balls with an ice-cream scoop. **Place** ice-cream balls in freezer to keep from melting.

2. Take ice-cream balls from freezer one at a time and roll each in crushed peppermint candy and shredded coconut (if desired).

3. Put each snowball back in freezer until ready **to** serve.

4. When ready to serve, put each one in a small dish **and** cover with chocolate sauce.

CORNFLAKE
KISSES

What could be nicer than
baking delicious Cornflake Kisses
for your friends?
With a grownup's help, perhaps
you can have a party!

WHAT YOU NEED

2 egg whites   2 cups cornflakes
¾ cup sugar   ½ teaspoon vanilla flavoring
       1 cup dry shredded coconut

WHAT TO DO

1. Beat the egg whites until they are stiff.
2. Gradually add the sugar, and keep beating!
3. Gently fold in the other ingredients, just barely mixing everything together.
4. Drop the batter onto a greased cookie sheet, a teaspoonful at a time.
5. Bake in a moderate oven (325°F) for 12 minutes.

(makes 30 small Kisses)

stan tuson

FRUIT KABOBS

Good snacks! Handy, too — just pass a plateful, no forks or spoons needed!

WHAT YOU NEED

8 maraschino cherries

8 pineapple chunks

8 miniature marshmallows

8 toothpicks

HOW TO FIX

1. For each toothpick, stick on one maraschino cherry, one pineapple chunk and one miniature marshmallow (like stringing beads).

2. Eat with your fingers. Please don't chew the toothpick!

This makes 2 servings.

LOLLI-COTS

Make your own lolli-cots. They taste better
than you-know-what, and — surprise!
— they're even good for you!

WHAT YOU NEED

Dried apricot halves
Pecan halves
Raw sugar

HOW TO FIX

1. Cook dried apricot halves in simmering (barely boiling) water until softened, about 7 to 10 minutes.
2. Drain on paper towel, and let cool for 15 minutes.
3. Wrap each apricot half around a pecan half.
4. Spread a little raw sugar in a saucer. Roll each apricot-pecan-pop in the sugar.
5. Spear each pop with a party pick, and serve on a plate.
This recipe makes one lolli-cot for each apricot half.

CINNAMON MOONS

You'll smile like the *Man in the Moon*
when you bite into a cinnamon moon.

WHAT YOU NEED:

  1 package refrigerated crescent rolls

  1 tablespoon soft butter or margarine

  2 tablespoons sugar

½ teaspoon cinnamon

HOW TO FIX:

1. Have an adult pre-heat oven to 375°.

2. Separate crescent rolls and spread soft butter on them with a knife.

3. Mix sugar and cinnamon in a small bowl. Then sprinkle over dough.

4. Roll up each roll, starting at the shortest side of each triangle. Curve ends to make each roll look like a crescent moon.

5. Place rolls on an ungreased cookie sheet.

6. Bake in oven for 12 to 15 minutes, until golden brown.

Then carefully remove from cookie sheet with a spatula. Makes 8 servings.

YOGURT-JAM POPS

For a cool and yummy treat,
make your own frozen yogurt-jam pops.

WHAT YOU NEED:

1 container (8 oz.) plain yogurt
3 tablespoons jam or preserves (your favorite flavor)
2 paper cups
2 wooden sticks or wooden spoons

HOW TO FIX:

1. Place yogurt and jam in a small mixing bowl. Mix together with a spoon.
2. Fill paper cups with the yogurt-jam mixture. Place a wooden stick or wooden spoon in the center of each cup.
3. Place filled cups in the freezer until mixture freezes.
4. When ready to eat, tear away the paper cup.

CHEERY
CHERRY COBBLER

Surprise your family
with this delicious desert.

WHAT YOU NEED:

1 package refrigerated biscuits
2 tablespoons butter or margarine, melted
2 tablespoons sugar
½ teaspoon cinnamon
1 can cherry pie filling
  Vanilla ice cream

HOW TO FIX

1. Ask Mother to help heat the oven to 375°F.
2. Separate biscuits and place them on an ungreased cookie sheet.
3. Brush melted butter over the biscuits.
4. Mix sugar and cinnamon together, then sprinkle over biscuits.
5. Bake in oven for 12 to 15 minutes, until golden brown.
6. While biscuits are baking, heat pie filling in a saucepan over low heat.
7. Place a biscuit in each dessert dish, then spoon cherry pie filling over the biscuit. Top with a scoop of vanilla ice cream.

This makes 8 servings

stan tusan

JAM TARTS

The Queen of Hearts would surely like
these yummy tarts, and so will you!

WHAT YOU NEED

1 package refrigerated big flaky biscuits
Jam or jelly

HOW TO FIX

1. Start heating oven to 375° F. Ask Mother to help.

2. Separate biscuits.

3. Dip bottom of small glass in flour, then press down center of each biscuit with glass.

4. Fill center of each biscuit with a spoonful of jam.

5. Place filled biscuits on baking sheet.

6. Bake in oven 15 minutes.

Let the tarts cool a bit so you won't burn your tongue!

DELUXE
DOUGHNUT SUNDAE

The chocolate sauce is topped by the nuts. The ice cream is topped by the chocolate sauce. But the doughnut is at the bottom of it all!

WHAT YOU NEED

1 Doughnut

1 Scoop vanilla ice cream

Chocolate sauce

Nuts (any kind you like or are allowed to munch)

HOW TO FIX

1. Place the doughnut in a dessert plate.
2. Put a scoop of vanilla ice cream right in the center of the doughnut (the hole, of course!).
3. Now pour a little chocolate sauce over the ice cream.
4. Top with a sprinkling of nuts.

This delicious dessert could be made up quickly as a party treat!

DOUGHNUT
CLOWN

For a spooky night or any time
this doughnut clown is fun to make
and so good to eat.

WHAT YOU NEED

Doughnut
Vanilla ice cream
Candy corn
Jumbo gumdrop

HOW TO FIX

1. Place doughnut on a dessert plate.
2. Put a scoop of ice cream in the center of the dough-nut.
3. Make a clown's face with candy corn, then put a gumdrop on top for his hat.

It's so easy you'll want to make one for a friend, too.

PAINTBRUSH
COOKIES

You'll be an artist when you make these cookies. It's **fun** to paint designs that you can bake and eat!

WHAT YOU NEED

1 package refrigerated sugar cookies
1 egg yolk
¼ teaspoon water
  Food coloring

HOW TO FIX

1. Start heating oven to 375° F.
2. Slice cookie roll in ¼-inch slices, then place slices on baking sheet 2 inches apart.
3. Mix egg yolk and water, then divide mixture into 4 small dishes.
4. Mix a drop of food coloring in each dish, making each one a different color.
5. Paint designs on cookies with a small clean paintbrush.
6. Bake painted cookies in oven 8 to 10 minutes.

Great fun for a rainy day — invite a friend to help.

PEACHY
DESSERT

On any sunny day
this peachy dessert
will bring smiles.

stan tusan

WHAT YOU NEED

6 canned peach halves
10 vanilla wafers
   Whipped topping (the kind that squirts from a can)

HOW TO FIX

1. Drain liquid off peaches.
2. Put wafers in paper bag, then crush with a rolling pin to make crumbs.
3. Pour crumbs into a bowl, then roll peach halves in crumbs.
4. Place peach halves in dessert dishes.
5. Squirt whipped topping on top of each peach.

FUDGY PUDDING POPS

Feel as cool as a snowball
when you munch a
fudgy pudding pop.

WHAT YOU NEED

1 package (about 4 oz.) instant chocolate pudding
2 cups milk
   Wooden sticks
   Paper cups

HOW TO FIX

1. Beat pudding mix and milk until smooth, about one minute.
2. Spoon pudding into paper cups.
3. Insert a wooden stick in each pudding pop.
4. Place in freezer until frozen solid.

To eat, just tear off the paper cup!

PEACH SUNDAE

A yummy treat that's
hard to beat is a sundae
made with peaches,
fresh ones or canned ones.

WHAT YOU NEED

1 scoop vanilla ice cream
½ of a peach
fresh raspberries or canned mixed fruit
a dessert bowl

HOW TO FIX

1. Place ½ of a peach in the dessert bowl.
2. Then, put the scoop of ice cream in the hollow part of the peach.
3. Pour raspberries or canned fruit over top of the ice cream .
4. Now, just cool off while enjoying the treat!

stan tusan

PUDDING CONES

For dessert or an afternoon snack
pudding cones are great to eat,
indoors or out!

WHAT YOU NEED

1 package (4 ozs.) instant pudding
(any flavor you like)

2 cups milk

8 ice cream cones

HOW TO FIX

1. Stir milk into pudding mix, beat 1 minute.

2. Set ice cream cones in a small glass to keep them from falling over.

3. Spoon pudding into cones, and they're ready to eat.

stan tusan

SNOW ON THE MOUNTAIN SUNDAE

A favorite combination
of flavors that
everyone will like!

WHAT YOU NEED:

4 slices pound cake

4 scoops ice cream

4 tablespoons chocolate syrup

Whipped cream or prepared dessert topping

HOW TO FIX:

1. Put a scoop of ice cream on each slice of cake.
2. Spoon 1 tablespoon chocolate syrup over each serving.
3. Top with whipped cream.

Makes 4 servings.

stan tusan

ISLAND DESSERT

Eating this may make you **feel**
like you are wearing a grass skirt
and dancing the hula.

WHAT YOU NEED:

1 can (20 oz.) pineapple chunks
40 miniature marshmallows
Shredded coconut

HOW TO FIX:

1. Open can of pineapple and pour into a bowl with juice.
2. Add marshmallows to pineapple.
3. Stir well.
4. Sprinkle coconut on top. Place in the refrigerator at least three hours or overnight.
5. Spoon into serving dishes.

Makes 4 to 5 servings.

stan tusan

SPOOKY PUDDINGS

A cat, a witch, a ghost and a jack-o'-lantern—
make these spooky-face puddings for Halloween.

stan tusan

WHAT YOU NEED:

1 package (3¾ ounces) instant vanilla pudding
2 cups cold milk
   Shredded coconut
   Maraschino cherries
   Raisins
   Peanuts

HOW TO FIX:

1. Prepare pudding with milk, as directed on the package.
2. Pour pudding into 4 dessert dishes. Set puddings in refrigerator to chill for 5 minutes.
3. To make spooky faces, use coconut for hair, cherry for nose, raisins for eyes, peanuts for a mouth. Make a different spooky face on each pudding.

This makes 4 desserts.

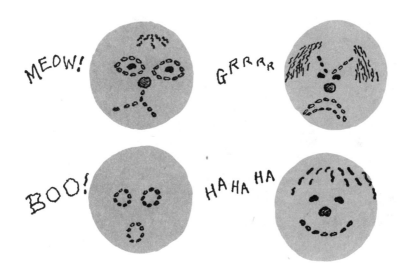

SPICY APRICOTS

Make this delicious dessert in the morning so it will be chilled by dinnertime!

WHAT YOU NEED

1 can (30 ounces) whole apricots
¼ cup honey
2 tablespoons vinegar
1 cinnamon stick
3 whole cloves

HOW TO FIX

1. Drain apricots, saving the syrup. Measure ½ cup of syrup to use.

2. Put the drained apricots into a serving dish.

3. In a small saucepan, mix together the honey, vinegar, cinnamon, cloves, and the syrup from step 1.

4. Heat the liquid mixture on the stove with your parent's help, until the mixture comes to a boil.

5. Pour this heated sauce over the apricots. Chill several hours in the refrigerator, and serve.

This recipe makes 6 servings.

stan tusan

Lunches, Brunches and Breakfasts

Now that you've had some experience making sandwiches and preparing tasty beverages, you're ready to try recipes that are a little harder. Several of the recipes in this section involve the use of the stove, broiler or toaster, so be sure your mother is there to give you a hand.

Although we have said that these recipes are for lunches or brunches or breakfasts, you can eat them any time you want to. Snacks don't always have to be ice cream, cookies or candy, you know. After spending a couple of hours splashing in a backyard pool, you may be hungry enough for Pizza Muffins. Or perhaps you have spent the afternoon building a snowman; then Mexican Tomato Broth would taste especially good.

Brunch is a made-up word. The *br* comes from breakfast and the *unch* from lunch. Does that give you a clue to the meaning of the word? That's right; brunch is a combination breakfast-lunch. The usual time is later than breakfast but earlier than lunch. Many people have brunch on Sunday; the family has more time to sit down together and enjoy a leisurely meal. Or maybe your mother invites some neighbors in for brunch during the week. You and your friends can have a brunch party, too. Just pick a recipe from this section and make enough for everyone you've invited. A mid-morning party can be every bit as much fun as one in the afternoon.

For a special treat, why not mix and fix breakfast for Mother?

Or serve Dad breakfast in bed on his birthday? Cooking for others is even more fun than cooking for yourself. To make certain that the recipe turns out the way it should, read it carefully and assemble all the ingredients before you start. Then, if you discover there's no cinnamon, for example, in the house, you can pick another recipe without having wasted any of your time or Mother's ingredients.

YOUNG CHILDREN'S MIX AND FIX COOKBOOK can be the first in your library of cookbooks. As you grow, you'll continue to discover the fun of cooking, and you'll go on to more complicated recipes. Regardless of where you are or how old you are or whether you're a boy or a girl, knowing how to cook is a valuable talent. Quite a few people make their living cooking; it can be a very satisfying career.

Great cooks aren't born; it's a skill that anyone can learn. Everyone should know how to follow a recipe and anyone who can read can cook. There's no magic involved; just practice.

Everybody has to eat, and those who know how to prepare their own meals and how to cook for family and friends will have developed a talent and skills that will be invaluable all life long. So welcome to the wonderful world of cooking; it can be as full of adventure as anything you can imagine!

TOASTY TREAT

Surprise your friends with this
special lunch treat.

WHAT YOU NEED

1 can condensed tomato soup
¼ cup milk
1 cup shredded Cheddar cheese
4 slices toast

HOW TO FIX

1. Place soup, milk and cheese in a saucepan. Stir with a wooden spoon.

2. Place saucepan on stove over low heat. Cook until cheese is melted, stirring with a wooden spoon.

3. Place one slice of toast on each plate, then pour sauce over toast.

Makes 4 servings.

PIZZA MUFFINS

Everybody's favorite lunch!
One sniff of that melting
goodness and you'll be
wild till it's ready to eat!

WHAT YOU NEED

2 English muffins
Butter or margarine
1/3 cup canned tomato sauce
Oregano
1/3 cup grated American cheese
Grated Parmesan cheese

HOW TO FIX

1. Ask a grown-up to start heating the broiler.
2. Split muffins, and toast lightly.
3. Spread each muffin half with butter, then with tomato sauce.
4. Sprinkle a dash of oregano on each half.
5. Sprinkle with American cheese, and add a dash of Parmesan cheese.
6. Place pizzas on broiler pan, and toast in broiler until cheese melts.

This makes 2 servings.

CRUNCHY APPLE TREAT

For breakfast, for a snack, or even dessert —
this is a good winter warm-up treat!

WHAT YOU NEED

½ cup apple sauce

¼ cup chopped walnuts

4 frozen waffles or slices of bread

HOW TO FIX

1. Mix the applesauce and walnuts in a small bowl.

2. If using waffles, toast in the toaster according to directions. If bread, toast as you usually would.

3. After toasting, spread with butter or margarine.

4. Spread with the apple-nut mixture. Eat right away while the treat is warm.

This makes 4 servings.

stan tusan

LITTLE PIZZAS

The butcher, the baker, the *pizza maker*—
Here's a recipe that will make you famous!

WHAT YOU NEED

2 English muffins
¼ cup catsup
¼ cup grated American cheese
1 frankfurter

HOW TO FIX

1. Ask Mother to start heating the broiler.
2. Split muffins in half, then toast them.
3. Spread each toasted muffin half with catsup, then sprinkle cheese on top.
4. Slice frankfurters like "coins" and place a few on top of each muffin.
5. Place pizzas on broiler pan.
6. Broil 1 minute, until cheese is melted. Makes **4** little pizzas.

ORANGE
HONEY TOAST

Surprise Mother
with this breakfast treat.

WHAT YOU NEED

2 tablespoons honey
¼ teaspoon grated orange peel
1 teaspoon orange juice
2 slices toasted bread

HOW TO FIX

1. Mix honey, orange peel and orange juice.
2. Spread on hot toasted bread.

Serve at once while it's still warm.

stantusan

CINNAMON TOAST

Here's a tasty and simple recipe,
one which can taste mighty good
in the morning . . .
or on a spooky night!

MUNCH
MUNCH
MUNCH

TRICK
OR
TREAT

WHAT YOU NEED

1 teaspoon cinnamon

Slice of bread

2 tablespoons sugar

Pat of butter

HOW TO FIX

1. Mix the sugar and cinnamon together.

2. Toast the bread, then butter it.

3. Now sprinkle the cinnamon-sugar mixture on top of the buttered toast.

There should be enough mixture for 4 slices of toast. Perhaps you'd like to fix a piece for someone else, too!

stan tusan

WALKING
BANANA
SALAD

For your next performance in the kitchen this recipe is just the ticket. It's made on a wooden stick like a frozen pop!

WHAT YOU NEED

1 banana

Mayonnaise

¼ cup chopped peanuts

2 wooden sticks

HOW TO FIX

1. Peel banana, then cut it in half crosswise.
2. Put wooden stick in end of each banana half.
3. Spread banana with mayonnaise.
4. Roll in chopped nuts.

Makes 2 — one for you, one for a friend.

CANDLESTICK SALAD

Here's a recipe for an easy salad that's pretty to look at, fun to make, good to eat!

stan tusan

WHAT YOU NEED

1 lettuce leaf

1 canned pineapple slice

1 small banana

1 maraschino cherry

HOW TO FIX

1. Place the lettuce leaf on a salad plate.

2. Now place the pineapple slice on the lettuce.

3. Stand the banana in the pineapple hole. Make sure the banana is cut flat on the bottom to stand straight.

4. Put the cherry on top of the banana to make the "flame." (A toothpick might help keep it in place.) What a nice birthday salad this could be!

MEXICAN TOMATO BROTH

A good warming-up soup! To be very
Mexican, call it *Caldo Con Tomates.*

WHAT YOU NEED:

1 can (13¾ ounces) beef broth
1 cup seasoned tomato juice
¼ teaspoon salt
⅛ teaspoon chili powder (leave this out if you don't like chili)
⅛ teaspoon oregano or thyme

HOW TO FIX:

1. Mix everything together in a saucepan.
2. Simmer 5 minutes on the stove. Your mother can help with the stove.
3. Serve warm in bowls or large cups. Serve with corn chips or saltine crackers.

Makes 3 cups.

stan tusan

CHRISTMAS
BREAKFAST SPREAD

Here's a surprise you can make yourself
and serve to your family
for a Christmas breakfast treat!

WHAT YOU NEED:

6 English muffins
Butter or margarine
1 can (you'll use less) jellied cranberry sauce
Brown sugar
Cinnamon

HOW TO FIX:

1. Toast halves of English muffins in the toaster, and butter them.
2. Spread the cranberry sauce on the muffin halves.
3. Sprinkle 1 to 2 teaspoons of brown sugar over the cranberry sauce.
4. Sprinkle a dash of cinnamon over the sauce.
5. Set the muffin halves on a large plate or platter, and serve with a "Merry Christmas!"
This makes 6 servings.

stan tusan